Get Up and Go
Being Active

How to Be Healthy!

by Amanda Doering Tourville   illustrated by Ronnie Rooney

PICTURE WINDOW BOOKS
Minneapolis, Minnesota

Special thanks to our advisers for their expertise:

Nora L. Howley, M.A., School Health Consultant
Silver Spring, Maryland

Terry Flaherty, Ph.D., Professor of English
Minnesota State University, Mankato

Editor: Christianne Jones
Designer: Tracy Davies
Page Production: Michelle Biedscheid
Art Director: Nathan Gassman
The illustrations in this book were created with
ink and watercolor.

Picture Window Books
151 Good Counsel Drive
P.O. Box 669
Mankato, MN 56002-0669
877-845-8392
www.picturewindowbooks.com

Printed in the United States of America.

All books published by Picture Window Books
are manufactured with paper containing at least
10 percent post-consumer waste.

Library of Congress Cataloging-in-Publication Data
Tourville, Amanda Doering, 1980–
Get up and go : being active / by Amanda Doering Tourville;
illustrated by Ronnie Rooney.
p. cm. — (How to be healthy!)
Includes index.
ISBN 978-1-4048-4811-5 (library binding)
1. Exercise for children—Juvenile literature. 2. Physical
fitness—Juvenile literature. I. Rooney, Ronnie. II. Title.
RJ133.T68 2008
613.7′1083—dc22   2008006419

Being active keeps your body and mind healthy. Exercise helps build strong muscles and bones. Being active is fun, and it makes you feel good. There are many ways to be active.

Juana and Maria walk to school instead of getting a ride.

They enjoy the fresh air and exercise.

At recess, Juana and her friends jump rope.

Maria and her friends climb on the playground equipment.

Sometimes they all play kickball.

Playing is being active. Have fun being active with your friends.

Maria's favorite class is physical education. She always joins in. Today, her class is playing softball.

After school, Juana goes to basketball practice.
Juana stretches her muscles before she plays.

She jogs around the gym
to warm up.

Always stretch your muscles and warm up
before exercising. Warm, loose muscles work
better than cold, tight muscles.

Maria and Juana walk home together.

Instead of waiting for the elevator in their apartment building, they take the stairs.

Even small things help you stay active. Dance to your favorite song or help clean the house.

13

14

The family needs milk for dinner. Juana and her mom ride their bikes to the store.

After dinner, Maria and her dad
take the dog for a walk.

At the park, Maria throws a stick for her dog to fetch.

Pets can help you be active. Play with your pet every day.

On Saturdays, Maria takes gymnastic lessons. She cartwheels across the mat.

She balances on the beam.

Kids should be active at least one hour every day.

In the summer, the family goes swimming.
Juana and Maria race across the pool.

They jump off the diving board.

In the winter, Juana and Maria put on their warmest clothes. They go outside and build a snow fort.

Juana and Maria have fun and stay active all year.

As long as you dress right, you can be active in any weather.

23

To Learn More

More Books to Read

Feeney, Kathy. *Get Moving: Tips on Exercise.*
    Mankato, Minn.: Bridgestone Books, 2002.
Rockwell, Lizzy. *The Busy Body Book: A Kid's Guide*
    to Fitness. New York: Crown Publishers, 2004.
Salzmann, Mary Elizabeth. *Being Active.* Edina,
    Minn.: Abdo Publishers, 2004.

On the Web

FactHound offers a safe, fun way to find Web sites related to topics in this book. All of the sites on FactHound have been researched by our staff.

1. Visit *www.facthound.com*
2. Type in this special code: 1404848118
3. Click on the FETCH IT button.

Your trusty FactHound will fetch the best sites for you!

Look for all of the books in the How to Be Healthy! series:

Index